My Canada
NORTHWEST TERRITORIES

By Sheila Yazdani

TABLE OF CONTENTS

A Crabtree Seedlings Book

Crabtree Publishing
crabtreebooks.com

School-to-Home Support for Caregivers and Teachers

This book helps children grow by letting them practice reading. Here are a few guiding questions to help the reader build his or her comprehension skills. Possible answers appear in red.

Before Reading:

• What do I know about Northwest Territories?
  • *I know that Northwest Territories is in northern Canada.*
  • *I know that it can be very cold in Northwest Territories.*

• What do I want to learn about Northwest Territories?
  • *I want to learn what activities I can do in Northwest Territories.*
  • *I want to learn what the official flag looks like.*

During Reading:

• What have I learned so far?
  • *I have learned that Yellowknife is the capital of Northwest Territories.*
  • *I have learned that Virginia Falls is 96 meters (315 feet) high.*

• I wonder why...
  • *I wonder why the official flower is the mountain avens.*
  • *I wonder why Yellowknife gets more hours of sunshine in the summer than anywhere else in Canada.*

After Reading:

• What did I learn about Northwest Territories?
  • *I have learned that you can catch huge lake trout at Point Lake.*
  • *I have learned that the official bird is the gyrfalcon.*

• Read the book again and look for the glossary words.
  • *I see the word **capital** on page 6, and the word **shield** on page 12. The other glossary words are found on pages 22 and 23.*

I live in Inuvik. It is next to a freshwater **delta**.

My town doesn't get much sun in December. Inuvik **celebrates** the return of the sun every January with the Sunrise Festival.

Yellowknife

Northwest Territories is a **territory** in northern Canada. The **capital** is Yellowknife.

Fun Fact: Yellowknife is the largest city in Northwest Territories.

The official bird is the gyrfalcon.

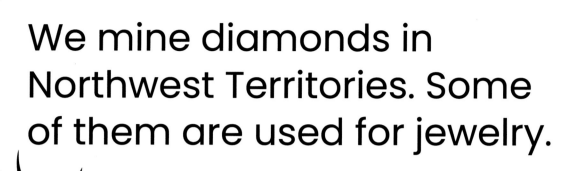

We mine diamonds in Northwest Territories. Some of them are used for jewelry.

Fun Fact: Eleven billion dollars of diamonds have been mined in Northwest Territories from 2014 to 2022.

My territory's flag is blue and white. There is a **shield** in the middle.

Yellowknife has more hours of sunshine in the summer than anywhere else in Canada.

I like to visit Nahanni National Park Reserve. I enjoy canoeing down the Nahanni River.

Fun Fact: Virginia Falls, in Nahanni National Park Reserve, is 96 meters (315 feet) high.

My family and I like to visit Wood Buffalo National Park so we can see the bison that live there.

The **northern lights** are beautiful to watch. The light looks like it is dancing across the night sky.

Fun Fact: The northern lights can be seen 240 nights of the year in Northwest Territories.

My friends and I go fishing on Great Bear Lake.